Home FUN booklet 5

Michela Capone

Letter to parents

Dear parents,

Welcome to *The Home Fun Booklet*! We hope you will use the activities inside to help your child practise English at home and with their friends.

Your child will bring home this booklet to practise with you what they have learned in class. You don't need to be an English expert to help your child with these activities. All the answers and audio recordings are online at http://www.cambridge.org/funresources . Have fun and keep practising with your child. Try to use the vocabulary here in everyday life and games and don't worry about making mistakes. On pages 7, 11, 15, 19 and 23 you will see this tree:

This tree shows how your child's knowledge will grow and progress through the units. Ask your child to read the 'I can…' sentences in the tree and to think about what they say. They can colour in the leaves green, orange or red when they agree – try to say 'Well done!'

The *Let's have fun!* pages (24–25) feature projects that develop language, mathematical, digital, social, learning and cultural skills useful for modern life. Look for the following signs next to activities in the booklet to show which of these skills your child is developing:

language

mathematics and science

digital

social and civic

learning to learn

culture

sense of initiative and entrepreneurial spirit

write/draw your own ideas

The picture dictionary at the end of the booklet (pages 26–31) is for your child to write in through the year. Ask them to write the words they know from all the topics. Make sure they can see they are progressing!

This booklet helps to prepare children for the Cambridge English: Young Learners tests, which are a great way to give your child more confidence in English and reward their learning. For more information, please go to: http://www.cambridgeenglish.org/exams/young-learners-english .

We hope both you and your child enjoy using this booklet and have fun!

The Cambridge Team

Download

the Word FUN World app

Contents

Michela Capone

Sports and leisure

eagle

spaceship

A Look and write.

1.
m u s i c

2.
_ e _

3.
_ _ a _ _

4.
_ a _ _ oo _

5.
_ a _ _ _ _

6.
_ e _ _

7.
_ i _ e   _ a _ e

8.
_ a _ e _ _ a _

9.
_ _ i _

B Complete with words from the box.

dancing   match   ~~hopping race~~   quiz   camping   party

running

one leg

hopping race

questions

prize

cake

birthday

competition

sport

forest

music

sleep

legs

4

C Look and read. Complete the words.

1. Shall we play **v** ...olleyball.. tonight?

2. Shall we go **c** .... at the weekend, William?

3. Shall we enter the **b** .... **r** .... on sports day?

4. Shall we dress up in a pirate **c** .... for Sophia's party?

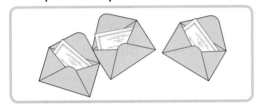

5. Shall we write **i** .... for the party, William?

6. Shall I take a **t** .... when we go camping?

7. Shall we read the new **m** .... that I bought from the shop, Sophia?

8. Shall we take an **u** .... ? It might rain.

D Work with a partner. Ask and answer the questions in exercise C. Invent new questions.

Shall we ...go to the volleyball match tomorrow.. ?

Shall we .... ?

Shall we .... ?

5

The world around us

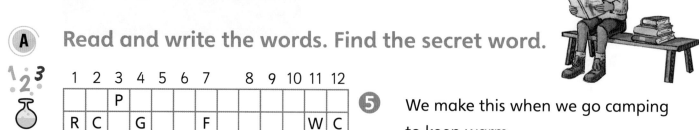

A Read and write the words. Find the secret word.

	1	2	3	4	5	6	7	8	9	10	11	12
			P									
	R	C		G			F				W	C
	A				F	G				W		
	I							S				
	N							W				

1. This is wet weather.
2. Another word for an 'animal'.
3. Putting a plant in the ground.
4. Another word for 'floor' but outside.
5. We make this when we go camping to keep warm.
6. This is green. It can grow in the garden.
7. This is a large green place. Animals live on it and plants grow here.
8. We live on this. It is another word for Earth.
9. This is the opposite of hard.
10. It is not hot. It is not cold. It is ....
11. This material comes from sheep.
12. This is the opposite of hot.

B Read and circle the correct answer.

1. Some dinosaurs always ate sweets / (plants).
2. It always rains in the **desert / jungle**.
3. Olives are never **black / blue**.
4. Wool never comes from a **sheep / horse**.
5. Vegetables sometimes grow in **the air / the ground**.
6. You can often start a fire with **wate / paper**.
7. The Earth has always been **round / square**.
8. A **silver / gold** cup is always the bes prize.
9. Camels never eat **chocolate / plants**
10. It is always sunny in **winter / summe** in Spain.

C Look at exercise B. Write a quiz and ask your family or friends.

The opposite of cold is warm / hot.
....
....
....
....

D Write two more questions and ask your family or friends.

How often do you plant flowers in your garden?

I never plant flowers in the garden. My mother does that.

	Name	Name	Name	Name	Name
How often do you eat vegetables?					
How often do you go out when it's raining?					
How often do you forget to take your rucksack to school?					
....					
....					

✔ I know sports and leisure words.

I can ask questions using *Shall we ...?*

I can read sentences about the natural world.

I can choose the correct answer in a quiz about the natural world.

I can ask questions and use *always, often, sometimes* and *never*.

= 😊

= 🙂

= 🙁

The body and the face

A Write and draw.

1
dahe
...........head..........

2
lderuohss
....

3
wbleo
....

4
eeskn
....

5
gersnfi
....

6
esto
....

7
eetht
....

B Look and write.

| hair | shoulder | arm | hand | leg |
| feet | neck | ear | ~~nose~~ | eye | mouth |

........nose........

8

C Look and cross out the wrong word.

1
nails
fingers
hand
~~knees~~

2
nose
ears
eyes
legs

3
shoulders
hair
foot
arm

4
toes
legs
feet
mouth

D Read and write. Ask your family or friends.

1 Emma likes to use her head when she plays football,
....doesn't she.... ? Yes, she does.. (✓)

2 Emma likes to eat cake with her hands, ... ?
.... (✗)

3 Emma has got big feet, ... ? .... (✓)

4 Emma is using her tennis racket, ... ? .... (✓)

5 Emma is not using her hands to play football, ... ?
.... (✗)

6 Emma doesn't like camping, ... ? .... (✗)

7 ....

8 ....

Animals

(A) Look and read.

The camel makes the horse happy because it is funny.

The swan makes the hippo angry because it is more beautiful.

The eagle makes the parrot unhappy because it is faster.

The butterfly makes the beetle sad because it can't fly.

The snake makes the snail afraid because it is dangerous.

The tiger makes the wolf worried because it is bigger.

Now answer the questions.

1	Which animal is dangerous?	..the snake..
2	Which animal makes the wolf worried?	....
3	Which animal makes the parrot unhappy?	....
4	Which animal is funny?	....
5	Which animal is beautiful?	....
6	Which animal gets angry?	....
7	Which animal makes the beetle sad?	....
8	Which animal is afraid of the snake?	....

(B) Go online and make a poster of an animal.

Go to www.cambridge.org/funresources !

C Look at the picture and choose the best title.

A A day at the zoo ☐ **B** The king's colours ☐ **C** The fun park ☐

D ▶ Listen and colour the animals.
02

○ I know body and face words.

○ I can label the body.

○ I can read about animals and answer questions about them.

○ I can write sentences about my favourite animal.

○ I can listen to someone talking about animals and colour the animals.

= ☺
= 😐
= ☹

Review

A Read and find the words.

Find three body and face words.

Find three colours.

Find three animals.

Find three sports and leisure words.

Find three natural world words.

Find two names.

F	I	N	G	E	R	Q	Q	N	S	T	T	N	M	M
O	P	I	Y	H	F	M	M	G	H	N	N	G	R	A
E	E	R	T	I	U	I	O	P	O	P	L	K	W	T
L	L	K	J	P	H	H	G	F	U	D	S	G	H	C
A	A	T	G	P	L	H	K	H	L	S	H	T	I	H
H	K	Y	E	O	F	R	J	R	D	V	B	E	T	O
J	W	I	L	L	I	A	M	L	E	F	I	G	E	L
F	J	H	B	H	E	H	L	P	R	T	R	R	C	N
G	Q	W	O	Z	L	X	M	U	K	J	D	N	B	E
T	H	U	W	B	D	D	X	R	Z	A	S	E	Q	T
G	C	A	M	E	L	N	I	P	A	R	T	Y	M	I
A	Q	E	R	N	W	O	O	L	I	T	O	P	T	M
Q	R	I	Y	N	M	T	U	E	S	O	P	H	I	A
P	W	W	C	R	E	A	T	U	R	E	S	O	U	O
X	D	O	R	A	N	G	E	K	P	L	Y	Z	X	W

B Read and write.

winter volleyball shoulder ~~camel~~ grey hole flags knees swan
gold planting camping elbow beetle purple ground invitation
head hippo red

Animals
......camel......

....

....

....

Colours
....

....

....

Body and face
....

....

....

The world around us
....

....

....

....

Sports and leisure
....

....

....

....

12

c **Read and write. Ask and answer the questions with your family or friends.**

1

How often do you play volleyball?

I sometimes play volleyball at the weekends.

2

Which animal makes the wolf worried?

A tiger makes the wolf worried.

3

What is your favourite time of year?

My favourite time of year is...............................

4

What is the word for 'floor' but outside?

It is...

5

Which sport can you play in a field?

In a field, you can play.................................

6

When you play football, what parts of the body do you use?

I usually use...

7

What will you do at the weekend?

I might...

8

What are five parts of the body?

....

9

Tell your friend about something that makes you happy.

....

10

What are the colours of the rainbow?

....

Places and directions

A Look and write.

1. s c h o o l

2. _ _ e _ i _ _

3. _ o _ _ o _ _ i _ e

4. _ o _ e

5. _ _ a _ i o _

6. _ o _ _ i _ a _

7. _ i _ _ _ e _ _ _ e

8. _ _ o _ _ _
_ _ a _ i u _

B Read and write.

| river | bridge | mountains | skyscrapers | ~~flat~~ | police station | shoe factory |

Richard lives in a small in town in England called Amble. He doesn't live in a house, he lives in a **1** ......flat...... . He has lived here since he was born. His father works in a **2** .... and he even made Robert a pair of shoes for his birthday last year! Although Richard lives in a small town, there are many **3** .... and his mother works in one of them. She works in an office on the fourth floor and sometimes Richard visits her when he doesn't go to school. He likes looking at the **4** .... opposite the office because there are a lot of policemen that go in and out. He wants to be a policeman when he grows up. If you go into the city centre, you can find many shops.

There are a lot of high **5** .... behind the town and Richard and his family often go hiking together in the summer. A **6** .... goes through the town centre and you can walk over it using the **7** ....
Richard loves his town and is very happy here.

C Write about your town.

....
....
....

D Look at the example. Create a map of your town. Direct your friend to different places.

How do I get from the hospital to the chemist?

If you want to go from the hospital to the chemist, you can go over the bridge, past the police station and turn left.

I can use 'if' when giving directions.

I know words for places.

= 😊

= 😐

= 🙁

I can read and write about places.

I can talk about my town.

I can create a map of my town.

Health

A Find and circle nine health words.

doctovettemperaturebandagehospitalstomachachemedicinesickheadache

B Look and complete the sentences.

1

Lara fell off her bike so she went to the ....hospital...........

The doctor put a .... on because she had a bad cut.

2
Lara was at school yesterday and had a .... so she called her mother and she gave her some ....

3
Lara studied on her computer all day yesterday and she had a .... so her mother gave her some water and told her to go to bed.

4

Lara's dog felt .... at the weekend so Lara and her mother took the dog to the ....

C Match the sentences with Lara's friends with the same problem.

A

D

E

F

1 Lara can't eat or use her teeth. She has to go to the dentist tomorrow. —————————————

2 Lara feels hot and wants to stay in bed all day.

3 Lara can't eat a lot of food and her stomach is very sore.

4 Lara can't study, because her head is very sore. She needs to take some medicine.

5 Lara didn't sleep last night, because she went to a party. She is very tired today.

6 Lara doesn't feel well, but she doesn't know what the problem is.

D Write sentences with the words in the box.

| feel better | doctor | toothache | X-ray | bandages | temperature | strong | headache |

1 ...I have a headache............ so I have to take some medicine.

2 .... so ....

3 .... so ....

4 .... so ....

E Play the guessing game with your family or friends.

I can't eat and I need to go to the dentist. What's the matter with me?

School

A Look and write what is missing in the second box.

1 ....
2 ....
3 ....
4 ....
5 ....
6 ....

B Read and answer the questions.

Dear Peter
How are you? I'm fine! I am doing a project today about different schools all over the world. Let me tell you about mine. My school is in the city centre. It is next to the police station and I see the police cars pass by every day. When I was young I walked to school with my best friend and I still do today. There are 30 students in my class. I have a different teacher for each subject. My favourite teacher is Mr Young because he is nice and teaches maths. I love maths! Every day, I pack my rucksack with my school things. Today, I have a pair of scissors, some glue, a dictionary and my geography book. That is because I am studying art, French and geography today. We have two breaks a day and we have an hour for lunch. We eat lunch in the dining room with our friends. I often have homework and I study at home for three hours a day. Tell me about your school!
Harry

1 Where is Harry's school?
in the city centre

2 What is next to his school?
....

3 Who does he walk to school with?
....

4 What is his favourite subject?
....

5 How many breaks does he have at school? ....

6 How many hours does he study at home a day? ....

C Write a letter to Harry about your school.

....

....

....

18

D ▶ **Listen and circle the things you hear.**
03

rubber

book

rucksack

photo

ruler

scissors

board

football socks

E ▶ **Listen again and answer the questions.**
04

1 What is Harry's favourite book? ..a history book..

2 What is Ben wearing today? ....

3 Why isn't Sophia at school? ....

4 What colour is Emma's rucksack? ....

5 What did William draw on the board? ....

I can use 'so' in a sentence.

I know words about health.

I can read and write about school life.

I can listen and answer questions about different people in the classroom.

= ☺

= ☺

= ☹

I know school words.

19

Work

A Look and write.

①

......artist......

②

....

③

....

④

....

⑤

....

⑥

....

B Complete the sentences with the words in the box.

manager   journalist   queen   photographer   ~~actor~~   mechanic   artist

① An ....actor....... works on TV or in the theatre and is often famous.
② A .... uses a camera and takes photos of people and places.
③ The .... lives in a castle and sometimes wears a crown.
④ A .... works in a garage. He or she fixes cars and motorbikes.
⑤ A .... writes news stories for newspapers and sometimes goes on TV.
⑥ An .... uses paint and paints pictures of places and people.
⑦ A .... works in a company and has lots of people working for him or her.

C Look at Katy. Draw and write about you.

Katy's going to be an artist.

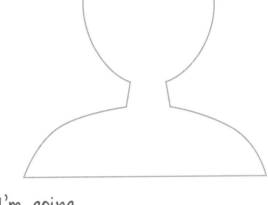

I'm going ....

....

D Read and play the game with your family or friends.

Actor

Do I work in a school?

Am I famous?

Do I work with people?

- Your friend writes a job on a piece of paper.
- Stick the paper on your forehead. Don't look at it!
- Ask your friend questions to guess the job. He or she must answer *yes* or *no*.
- If you can't guess, ask the final question, *What am I going to be?*
- Use these jobs: actor, mechanic, journalist, manager, photographer, queen, artist, designer.

21

Review

A Match and colour the second part of the sentences.

I had to buy a stamp because I wanted to send a letter to Marco in Italy so	my mum took me to the hospital to see a doctor.
My mum can't start her car and she said she can't take me to school. My dad told her to	I look in a dictionary.
I was playing in the garden and I fell over and cut my leg so	I went to the post office in town.
I love painting and drawing and at school my favourite subject was art, and	she bought me some medicine from the chemist.
I had a really bad headache and I was at school, I phoned my mum and	the vet.
When I study at school and at home, I sometimes don't know a word so	take it to the mechanic tomorrow morning.
When my dog was sick we took him to	the doctors took an X-ray and I could see my bones.
When I broke my leg last year, I went to the hospital and	now I am an artist and sell my paintings.

B Look and write a sentence.

1  I put my school things in my rucksack every day.

2  ....

3 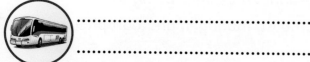 ....

4 ....

5  ....

6  ....

c Answer the questions and play noughts and crosses with your family or friends. Try to get a line ➜ or ↓!

I choose: What's a journalist? It's a person who writes about the news.

Great! I'm putting a cross in the box. Now your turn.

Correct!

OK. I choose ...

Where do you go if you need medicine?	What's a skyscraper?	If you eat too much food, what can happen?	What's a journalist?	What's a manager?
What do you use to cut things?	This person works in the theatre.	This person works with cars.	I feel sick so I go to the ...	Children go to this place from Monday to Friday and they study here.
What are you going to do in the future?	When was the last time you went to hospital?	What's your favourite place in your town?	You sit on these in the classroom.	You wear these on your feet when you play football.
Describe 'tired'.	Name two school subjects.	Name four things in your rucksack.	What's your favourite subject at school?	Who's your favourite teacher?
Describe your town.	You do this at home after school. Your teacher gives it to you.	You take this when you are sick.	Your body feels hot and you feel sick. What's the matter?	Where do you go to catch a train?

○ I can write sentences about what I am going to do in the future.

○ I know words for jobs.

= 😊

= 😐

= 🙁

○ I can guess a job from a description.

○ I can make sentences about jobs.

○ I can answer questions when playing a game.

Let's have fun!

(A) Play the board game with your family or friends.

Start

What's the opposite of hard?

What season comes after autumn?

Move on two squares.

Say three things about your town.

Point to your elbows.

Go back to Start.

Go back three squares.

What do you do at the weekend?

Touch your toes.

Say three colours.

Which animal makes a parrot unhappy?

I feel hot and I want to stay in bed. What's the matter with me?

This person helps animals when they are ill.

Finish

This person wears a crown.

Go to Finish.

In this subject, you learn about the world.

B Close your eyes and point to a word in each circle. Invent a sentence.

I am going to hospital tomorrow because I might need an X-ray......

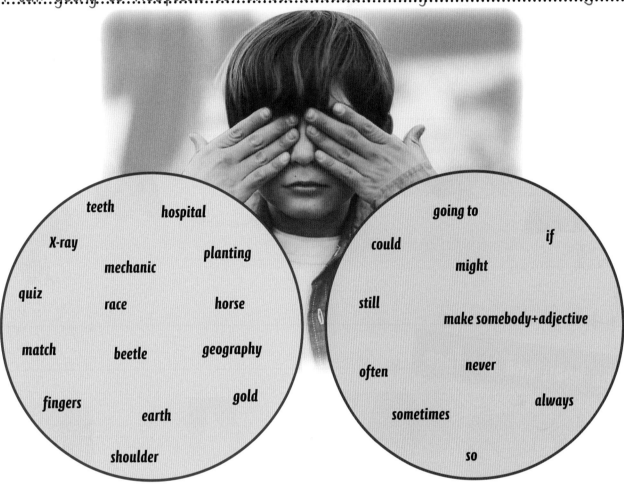

teeth   hospital

X-ray

planting

mechanic

quiz

race   horse

match   beetle   geography

fingers   gold

earth

shoulder

going to

could   if

might

still

make somebody+adjective

often   never

always

sometimes

so

C Make a video about your hobbies.

I love playing hockey, but I need to wear a helmet.

I play tennis with my friend, David.

Picture dictionary

Animals

....beetle....

....elbow....

The body and the face

Clothes

....belt....

Food and drink

.....biscuit.....

....

....

....

....

....

....

....

....

....

....

....

Health

.....bandage.....

....

....

....

The home

.....brush.....

....

....

....

....

....

....

....

....

Places and buildings

...airport...

....

....

....

....

....

....

....

....

....

....

....

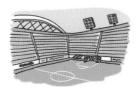
....

....

....

School

.backpack.

....

....

....

....

....

....

....

....

....

....

....

....

....

....

....

....

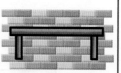
....

....

....

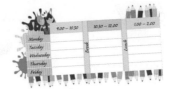
....

....

Sports and leisure

.rucksack.

....

....

....

....

....

....

....

....

....

....

....

....

....

....

....

....

....

....

....

....

....

....

....

....

....

....

....

....

....

....

....

....

....

Transport

....airport... ....

....

Work

.....actor..... ....

....

....

....

....

.....bridge.....

....

....

....

....

....

....

....

....

....

....

....

....

....

....

....

....

Acknowledgements

The author would like to thank her friends and colleagues at the British Council, Naples, for their support.

Design and typeset by Wild Apple Design.

Cover design and header artwork by Chris Saunders (Astound).

Audio production by Hart McLeod, Cambridge.

The authors and publishers acknowledge the following sources of copyright material and are grateful for the permissions granted. While every effort has been made, it has not always been possible to identify the sources of all the material used, or to trace all copyright holders. If any omissions are brought to our notice, we will be happy to include the appropriate acknowledgements on reprinting and in the next update to the digital edition, as applicable.

The publishers are grateful to the following for permission to reproduce copyright photographs and material:
Key: T = Top, B = Below

p. 25 (T): Adriana Varela Photography/Moment/ Getty Images; p. 25 (B): Adam Hester/Stockbyte/ Getty Images.

The authors and publishers are grateful to the following illustrators:
Akbar Ali (The Organisation) pp. 4 (TV), 29 (TV, member); Andrejs Ricci (The organisation) pp. 4 (music), 5 (towel, magazine), 18 (paper, board, rubber), 28 (screen), 29 (magazine), 31 (entrance, ocean); Andrew Painter (Sylvie Poggio Artists Agency) pp. 29 (concert, football match); Andy Elkerton (Sylvie Poggio Artists Agency) pp. 10 (camel, beetle, snail), 11 (swan, butterflies, donkey, beetle), 26 (beetle, butterfly, camel, fur, tortoise, elbow, toe, finger); Anthony rule pp. 4 (tent), 30 (airport, taxi), 31 (fire); Brett Hudson (Graham-Cameron Illustration) pp. 29 (instrument), 31 (stream); Bridget Dowty (Graham-Cameron Illustration) pp. 18 (dictionary), 27 (pizza), 27 (brush, cooker), 28 (castle, restaurant, bin, dictionary, glue, scissors), 30 (office); Chris Embleton-Hall (Advocate Art) pp. 18 (book, glue, scissors, pen, ruler, pencil), 28 (geography, gym, history, language, maths, project, science, shelf, student), 29 (diary, torch); Daniela Geremia (Beehive Illustration) pp. 28 (skyscraper); David Banks pp. 22 (timetable), 28 (timetable), 30 (fire fighter), 31 (earth, planet); David Sones (Sylvie Poggio Artists

Agency) pp. 14 (school), 26 (knees), 29 (chess, drum, golf, hotel, violin, volleyball), 30 (taxi); Galia Bernstein (NB illustration) pp. 16 (Lara), 17 (lady at desk, lion and Lara in cave), 23 (Lara); Gustavo Mazali (Beehive Illustration) pp. 20 (queen), 21 (art supplies), 26 (crown), 30 (astronaut, fire engine, queen, singer); Harriet Stanes (NB Illustration) pp. 26 (belt); Jamie Pogue (The Bright Agency) pp. 10 (tiger), 14 (house), 31 (desert); Johanna A Boccardo (Sylvie Poggio Artists Agency) pp. 29 (festival); John Haslam pp. 4 (calendar), 5 (umbrella), 10 (eagle, swan, butterfly), 11 (eagle), 14 (chemist, city centre, hospital, post office, rail station), 18 (computer), 22 (chemist), 22 (eagle, butterfly, insect, octopus, swan, butterfly, glove, ring, sunglasses, trainers, umbrella), 27 (chemist, stamp), 28 (factory, London, museum, post office, university), 29 (snowboard, tent, tyre, umbrella), 30 (platform, wheel), 31 (cave); Laetitia Aynié (Sylvie Poggio Artists Agency) pp. 29 (rock music), 31 (castle, exit); Lisa Smith pp. 27 (chopsticks, fork, knife, spoon); Mark Beech (NB illustration) pp. 14 (Robert getting on a bus, town), 15 (boy, girl), 23 (Robert), 27 (envelope, letter); Matt Ward (Beehive illustration) pp. 14 (stadium), 28 (bridge, hotel, stadium), 30 (factory), 31 (bridge); Melanie Sharp (Sylvie Poggio Artists Agency) pp. 4 (monsters playing basketball, party), 16 (boy green), 17 (green face), 18 (rucksack), 22 (rucksack), 26 (creature), 27 (boy green), 28 (bus stop, backpack, rucksack, study), 29 (backpack, cartoon, pop music, snowman, theatre stage), 30 (rocket), 31 (gate, hill); Nigel Kitching (Sylvie Poggio Artists Agency) pp. 16 (bandage, headache, stomach ache), 17 (tired, stomach ache, temperature, toothache, headache), 22 (toothache), 27 (bandage); Nina de Polonia (Advocate Art) pp. 5 (camping), 9 (hand, girl), 6 (hospital), 26 (dinosaur), 27 (butter), 29 (invitation), 30 (newspaper); Pablo Gallego pp. 28 (flag), 30 (waiter); Pip Sampson pp. 5 (Pirate costumes, invitations), 9 (bottom half, top half), 28 (online), 29 (online, sledge, snowball, snowboarding), 30 (spaceship), 31 (pyramid, space, wood, view); Pulsar Studios pp. 4 (quiz), 22 (bus), 28 (airport, police station), 29 (quiz), 30 (airport, police station); Roland Dry (Beehive Illustration) pp. 6 (Ben reading by the fire), 7 (ben's face, girl), 13 (Ben); Sarah Warburton pp. 4 (net), 5 (volleyball), 8 (boy holding bag), 9 (Emma on the beach), 27 (swing), 30 (bicycle); Sue Woollatt pp. 29 (ski); Tatio Viana (Advocate Art) pp. 4 (bike race), 5 (bike race), 20 (artist, mechanic, actor, journalist, photographer), 22 (photographer), 29 (suitcase), 30 (actor, artist, astronaut, journalist, business woman, engineer, mechanic, photographer, police officer).